Milly, Molly and the Sun Hat

"We may look different
but we feel the same."

It was summer again.
Milly and Molly had just finished their
picnic when a big, brown, straw sun hat blew
along the beach towards them.

"I wonder who owns it?" said Milly.
"Come on, let's find out," suggested Molly.

They didn't need to ask the two boys digging
bunkers in the sand. They could just see the
tops of their sun hats. It wasn't theirs.

They didn't need to ask the fisherman
sitting on a rock. He had his hat pulled tightly
down over his ears. It wasn't his.

They didn't need to ask the lady filling her basket with seaweed. She had her hand firmly on the top of her hat. It wasn't hers.

They didn't need to ask the little girls building castles in the sand. They had their hats tied under their chins. It wasn't theirs.

They didn't need to ask the sunbathers with busy feet. They were under a striped umbrella. It couldn't be theirs.

They didn't need to ask the old man with
a knobbly stick. He had wild hair escaping from
under his beanie. It wasn't his.

They didn't need to ask the windsurfers.
They had zinc on their noses and wind
in their ears. It wouldn't be theirs.

But what about the four snorklers?
There were four pairs of boots but
only three sun hats!

Milly and Molly slipped the big, brown, straw
sun hat under the fourth pair of boots and ran
all the way back to their picnic basket.

They passed lots of people
on the way home, some with sun hats
and some without.
"I hope we found the right owner," said Milly.